THE SECRET IS IN SURRENDER

Bearing the Fruit of a Healthy Marriage

Kim Perry

Copyright © 2022 by **Kim Perry**

All rights reserved. No part of this publication may be reproduced, distributed or transmitted in any form or by any means, without prior written permission.

www.kimperrywrites.com

Cover Design: Holli Snell

Back Cover Photo Credit: Nicole DeCarlo Fusan

Book Layout: Rob Perry

The Secret is in Surrender / Kim Perry. -- 1st ed.
ISBN 979-8-9864825-0-7

Dedicated to Rob.
Without you, there would be no "Us."
I am grateful for you and
I love being married to you.
You are the best example I know of
walking in surrender to the Holy Spirit.
Thank you for loving me well and for
making me laugh every day!

CONTENTS

ACKNOWLEDGMENTS 1
PREFACE 3
HOW TO USE THIS BOOK 5
INTRODUCTION 7
LOVE 13
JOY 19
PEACE 25
PATIENCE 31
KINDNESS 37
GOODNESS 43
FAITHFULNESS 49
GENTLENESS 53
SELF-CONTROL 59
WE ARE JUST BEGINNING 63
THE MOST IMPORTANT SURRENDER 65

ACKNOWLEDGMENTS

I have felt the pull to write a book for a long time. The proposed topic changed with each season of our lives, and I let the busyness of each season get in the way of completing the project. When it came down to it, this book is the result of simply setting aside time to write each day. The Lord directed the whole thing (I didn't even want to write this one when I started!) But I guess it makes sense that God would pull a book about marriage out of me. Besides being a daughter and sister, being a wife is my longest "gig!"

Rob Perry is an amazing husband, dad, pastor, and friend - he's good at "all the things," and he also is a great encourager. Thank you, Rob, for your steadfastness in championing my writing, and for all the time you spent helping me with this project and making it so much better. I could not have done this without you.

Thank you to my parents, Joan and Russ Page and Rob's parents, Elaine and Bob Perry. You have all modeled for us what it means to have a life-long marriage. We are so grateful.

Thank you to our children, Elizabeth and Nick, and their spouses, Will and Molly. I notice how well you love one another and I am insanely happy to be learning from you. You are all amazing people and I love you!

Thank you to Cindi Whiteside and Erika Close, for your kindness in proofreading the book, for offering gentle and constructive feedback, and for finding typos I had missed! I've made some edits and additions since then, so all the mistakes that remain are totally on me!

Many others have supported me in this endeavor, even if they weren't aware. To friends who commented on my blog posts - you have no idea how much that meant to me. Thanks to Matt Didway, for sharing your daily habit of "Matt, Inc." The working title of this book was "Kim, Inc." because I had no idea where it might land. Thanks to Diana Bowman, for your "just in the nick of time" encouragement - what a delight it was to find that we were working on book projects at the same time! And to Jan Limiero and the sweet circle of women that were my "True You" classmates during the pandemic, thank you all for believing that I could do this!

PREFACE

It's safe to say that we all want a better marriage. (At least, all who would venture to read this.) I believe that when it comes down to it, most of us are willing to do whatever it takes. Sometimes it is really difficult work. And sometimes, there are simple things that we have well within our reach that can make a huge difference toward a happier marriage.

Drs. Les and Leslie Parrott, renowned relationship experts who have helped countless marriages get off on the right foot and stay healthy say, "Marriage doesn't make you happy. You make your marriage happy." My husband, Rob, and I have been married 34 years to date and we can both vouch for that.

When people ask about the secret to our long-time marriage, we can't help but give God credit. He's the one who brought us together, and He's the one who has helped us stay together. But it's not all up to God, is it? Otherwise, every marriage would last. Wives and husbands have our part to play in it. Sometimes our part is obedience to God's calling. Sometimes, it's pure grit and determination. When the Holy Spirit is involved, He will supply all the power that is needed. As married people, the very best thing we can do is to humble ourselves and let that Power do its work.

I don't claim to be a relationship expert, but I have learned some things during all these years as a married person. This book is a way of capturing some of the wisdom gained, and owning the fact that I am still learning! Rob and I have mentored many couples and observed even more marriages over the years. We've found that when we help others prepare for or improve their marriage, we learn from them, so our relationship also gets better. Specific examples (good and bad) contained here are from our marriage, so if they bear resemblance to your relationship, that is simply because we have common struggles. I'm not airing anyone else's laundry here.

I hope that this resource will challenge and encourage us in our quest for better marriages. Let's lean in and let the Holy Spirit supply the roadmap and the power. I wholeheartedly believe that as we learn to love our spouses better, we will also learn to love all the people in our lives better as well. It's going to be great!

I am praying for your marriage even now.

HOW TO USE THIS BOOK

Whether you work through this as a couple or on your own, focus on your part of what needs to be done. Your marriage will improve even when only one of you does the work of seeking and yielding to the Holy Spirit. Seek Jesus for the sake of seeking Jesus, not to get your spouse to change. I hope you'll make this journey to glorify God, look more like Jesus, and honor the covenant YOU made to God and your spouse.

Weekly Study

Focus on one attribute each week. You'll likely be able to read, look up the verses, discuss your answers to the questions, and pray together in less than an hour. If you are in a season where things are strained or difficult between you, consider setting the simple goal of having a peaceful, loving conversation. Decide in advance that when things get tricky, or the discussion moves from a place of peace to a place of pain, you'll simply take a break. There is no hurry. Take as long as you need.

Retreat

If you have time to get away together for a few days or a week, divide the chapters over the time you have, being sure that you also make time for fun and relaxation. What do the two of you enjoy? Is it time in nature, exploring historic sites or unique shops? Good food? Coffee shops? Music festivals? Extreme sports? Whatever it is, be sure to make time for those things, as well. Create a culture of intimacy between you so that you both feel safe sharing at a heart level.

Premarital Devotional

If you are dating and want to work through this study together, it may set the groundwork for a more vibrant and rewarding future together. If you are engaged, use this to help you prepare for your marriage. I believe that all the questions will still apply; you may want to answer them more from a standpoint of dreaming together and setting goals for the marriage you hope to have. I encourage you to also find a mentor couple who can walk alongside you as you prepare your hearts for this life-long journey of commitment and learning. Marriage is truly the adventure of a lifetime! Remember, all worthwhile adventures entail some challenges.

INTRODUCTION

P aul wrote these words in his letter to the people in Galatia.

Galatians 5:22-23

But the Holy Spirit produces this kind of fruit in our lives: love, joy, peace, patience, kindness, goodness, faithfulness, gentleness, and self-control. There is no law against these things!

That's from the New Living Translation. These well-known verses offer guidance and hope for a better way of living and loving. Jesus made a way for us to have a relationship with God the Father and those who follow him receive the Holy Spirit as a gift. It is the Holy Spirit who produces the fruit in our lives. The Holy Spirit empowers us to exhibit these attributes. Trying to do this on our own would be an exercise in futility. But we are not on our own! God is here to help us.

I love words, so I'm always interested in comparing different versions of Scripture. Here are those same verses, expressed in a few other ways.

Amplified Bible

But the fruit of the Spirit [the result of His presence within us] is love [unselfish concern for others], joy, [inner] peace, patience [not the ability to wait, but how we act while waiting], kindness, goodness, faithfulness, gentleness, self-control. Against such things there is no law.

The Message

But what happens when we live God's way? He brings gifts into our lives, much the same way that fruit appears in an orchard—things like affection for others, exuberance about life, serenity. We develop a willingness to stick with things, a sense of compassion in the heart, and a conviction that a basic holiness permeates things and people. We find ourselves involved in loyal commitments, not needing to force our way in life, able to marshal and direct our energies wisely.

Look over the Scripture from Galatians again. Do you notice the way it begins?
"But the..."
Is it significant that this passage begins with "But the...?" You bet.
Here's what Paul is addressing just before we get to the famous list regarding the fruit of the Spirit:

Galatians 5:19-21:

When you follow the desires of your sinful nature, the results are very clear: sexual immorality, impurity, lustful pleasures, idolatry, sorcery, hostility, quarreling, jealousy, outbursts of anger, selfish ambition, dissension, division, envy, drunkenness, wild parties, and other sins like these. Let me tell you again, as I have before, that anyone living that sort of life will not inherit the Kingdom of God.

That's a pretty heavy list, isn't it?! This list could be called the "fruit of our flesh." I'm guessing that all of us have experience with at least a few of these, like hostility, quarreling, jealousy, angry outbursts, and selfish ambition. (And maybe just in the last hour!) When we are not intentional about surrendering to the Holy Spirit, this "flesh-fruit" will be ever-present in our lives.

Before we launch into a deeper look at the fruit of the Spirit, will you join me in taking a good hard look in the mirror? (It doesn't have to be weird. You look at you, and I'll look at me.) Ask God to show you how you are exhibiting this "flesh-fruit" in your life, in your marriage. He'll do it. My experience is that when I humble myself and ask for His help to see where I can improve, He is gentle. When I am prideful, though, feeling justified in my attitudes and behaviors, that's when I am choosing to learn "the hard way." You pick which way you want to go - choose your own adventure!

Anyway, what is important is that this list in verses 19-21 needs to be acknowledged and addressed. These should have no place in our marriages. As we grow in our understanding of God's love, of the lengths He has gone to forgive us so we can live a new way, our desire to be "done" with these things will also grow. Let's 'fess up to not being perfect. Let's bravely circle one or two things from the list that we already know we need God's help with. As we journey through these chapters, I believe we'll be replacing these bad habits, these "flesh-fruit" holdouts of our sinful nature, with the fruit of the Spirit. I pray that we'll keep at it until all that can be seen when we consider our marriage is a healthy luscious fruit of the Father's design.

Read the Passage Again

> *Galatians 5:22-23 But the Holy Spirit produces this kind of fruit in our lives: love, joy, peace, patience, kindness, goodness, faithfulness, gentleness, and self-control. There is no law against these things!*

The order of the list - does it matter? I am not a theologian, but I see a pattern. Love is listed first - it is the most obvious way to live like Jesus. It's the easiest and most basic on the list. You can't do any of the other things without Love. (Well, you might be able to try, but you will likely give up before you get through them all.) So, begin with Love. God is always first and best when it comes to Love.

1 John 4:19

We love each other because he loved us first. (NLT)

The first three qualities that the Holy Spirit produces in us are Love, Joy, and Peace. These seem to be focused on us - they are inward. They benefit our hearts, minds, and souls first, even as we live in such a way that the benefit extends to those around us.

Isn't it just like God, to make sure we are taken care of as we seek to represent Him well? Don't miss this opportunity! Allow the Holy Spirit to fill you up and meet your needs. Then the rest of the attributes in the list are more likely to be attainable.

The focus of the next four is more outward. Their impact is on people around us: Patience, Kindness, Goodness, and Faithfulness. And then the most difficult to master (at least, for me) are listed last. These require us to be wholly dependent on the Holy Spirit's help: gentleness and self-control.

While there is simplicity here, there is also a bit of mystery. You may have noticed that it's "fruit," singular. It is not "fruits" of the Spirit, like a grocery list you can pick and choose from. It is more like a perfectly blended fruit salad - each bite tasting more delicious and having a greater flavor profile than one single fruit has on its own. The flavors mix and mingle and enhance each other. As such, I cannot decide that since I've got Love and Joy "locked down" I can stop there. As long as all of these characteristics are not fully present in me, I still have work to do in becoming more like Jesus. The work is in submitting to the Holy Spirit; allowing Him to produce ALL the fruit. It should be noted that this is a lifetime endeavor! We will always have room to grow. Some characteristics will come more naturally to us and some will be more challenging. Since we have human brains, it will be more helpful to focus on one characteristic at a time, but let's remember that the goal is the whole mix.

Improving in one area will also help us make headway in some of the others. More mystery! But perhaps the most exciting mystery here is how we will be able to get there. We're going to need to struggle to the point of surrender. We'll need to wrestle our flesh, our desires, and our wills to the ground. Maybe even *into* the ground - put them to death in surrender to the Holy Spirit. Once our "selves" are out of the way, the Spirit will be free to counsel, guide, and direct us in the way we should go and empower us to put these things into practice. It will be as natural and automatic as breathing.

Living by the Spirit and having our lives marked by the fruit of the Spirit is not something we can do *without* the Spirit. When we trusted Christ for salvation, we were given the Holy Spirit as a gift - a deposit of what is to come. "It is God who enables us, along with you, to stand firm for Christ. He has commissioned us, and He has identified us as His own by placing the Holy Spirit in our hearts as the first installment that guarantees everything He has promised us." (2 Corinthians 1:21-22)

I have been a follower of Jesus since I was very young; almost 50 years at this point. That's a lot of years. During that time, I have grown in my understanding and in my relationship with God. I have also grown in my understanding *of* my relationship with God. Even as someone who is daily seeking God and learning to live and love more like Jesus, I am still a work in progress when it comes to living in the Spirit. Sure, there is a lot of healthy "Spirit fruit" in my life, but there is also a good amount of fleshly selfishness. Even after all these years of knowing God and walking with Him, my fleshly instinct, my gut reaction is to fight for and protect that which I feel is "rightfully mine." And while I generally end up making the Spirit-driven choice in the end, I am aware of the struggle. This kind of living is counter-cultural. It is counterintuitive, and counter to our nature. Our part is to pray daily for the Spirit to fill and guide us and then to surrender.

Another essential is to stay connected in community with people who will walk alongside you and encourage your faith and champion your marriage. We all need that kind of acceptance, accountability, and support for the journey.

If you have not yet decided to follow Jesus and accept the gift He offers (forgiveness, eternal life, his presence in your life through the Holy Spirit), I invite you to explore this book with the hope that God is real, that He loves you, and that He can help you make your marriage better. I hope you will check out the resources on **page 65** that will give you some more information about the Gospel.

Chapter One

LOVE

Um, yeah, of course, "Love." Is that even in question? Well, yes. It is. Because Love is so much more than the feeling of euphoria you felt when you first met, or got engaged, or left your wedding celebration and headed into your honeymoon. Those feelings are wonderful - and the attraction you feel for one another can be nurtured and stay healthy for the entirety of your lifelong marriage if you work at it. But feelings are unreliable. Feelings fade when the going gets tough. Inevitably, there will come a day (or maybe just a misguided few hours) when you will look at your spouse and question your decision. He might be wearing a food-stained t-shirt and picking his toenails. Her breath may be absolutely foul from the garlic-heavy lunch she ate with work friends. She may have just told you something you did not like hearing about how your family or friends treated her and how she felt about it. He may have stolen something off your plate that you were saving for last because it was your favorite bite. That's when you'll understand that Love is a conscious decision and action, not a feeling.

Loving well for your lifetime together is going to take resolve, energy, and more grit than you can imagine. It will require you to put yourself and your desires aside for the sake of your marriage. There will be heavy lifting. You will have some difficult days. You may even have a difficult decade.

Take heart! Because of your identity in Christ, you can love well even in trying times. Empowered by the Holy Spirit, you are not a slave to your selfish nature any longer. You are freed up to love one another the way Jesus loves - with selfless abandon.

Love gets out of bed to check that the front door is locked. Love makes dinner after a long day. Love offers to stop and pick up whatever's needed from the grocery store for making dinner - or offers to pick up dinner on the way home upon hearing it was a long day. Love runs out to the store when a crucial ingredient is missing. Love irons shirts. Love gives a backrub even when we are tired. Love empties the dishwasher instead of closing the door quickly when discovering the dishes are clean. Love means putting our own needs second, again. Love refrains from saying "I told you so." Love listens to the long description of a bad day when we've also had a bad day. Love helps us keep going past when we're tired. Love helps sweep up a broken dish that shattered and runs for paper towels when a drink is spilled.

Love holds its tongue even when harsh words seem justified. Love finds a way to discuss issues with grace and a soft tone. Love keeps going through hurt, betrayal, illness and the darkest days.

Love helps us serve one another well because Love is the choice to act, not a warm and fuzzy feeling. Deciding to actively love well is a choice to make today and every day. To be honest, we may try hard for a lifetime and still not get it right, because we are selfish by nature. But the Holy Spirit will be our guide, because God is Love, and we can look to Him for strength... and then ask for His forgiveness (and our spouse's) when we get it wrong.

We have gotten it wrong:

In our first year of marriage, we lived in a tiny apartment in Suburban Maryland. It was a one-bedroom with a den that we used mainly as an office, but also as a place for overnight guests to stash their suitcases since the guest bed was a pullout sofa in the adjacent living room. Rob's father and brother spent a night with us on their trip from Massachusetts to North Carolina when John was beginning his freshman year of college. As you might imagine, there was a lot on their minds. I know now, after dropping our children off at college, that there is a "special kind of tired" resulting from the packing and deciding, the keeping-details-straight, and the managing of emotions.

We had a great visit with them and after we sent them on their way in the morning, I started looking for the work folder that I had brought home because I had a client presentation with my boss first thing on Monday morning that I needed to prepare for. The folder was NOT where I left it. I checked everywhere, before realizing that my father-in-law, Bob, might have grabbed it up with his own files when they packed up.

This was before cell phones. I was an entry-level account manager with no authority. Rescheduling the client presentation was not an option. My boss was demanding and harsh and would have fired me for embarrassing him by inconveniencing his client. I did not handle this situation in a loving way. Quite the opposite. Nearly 33 years later, I clearly remember the fit I threw when Rob asked me "Do you *really* need the file this weekend?" and how justified I felt in doing so.

Thankfully, Love was active, even when I was at my worst. Rob showed Love by jumping through hoops (this was also before the internet!) to contact the hotel where his dad was staying that night and make sure there was a message for them when they checked in. And Bob showed me Love by driving to the nearest airport to send the folder back to me via air freight, even though he had truly important things to do with his son's college drop-off. I was able to pick up the folder very early on Monday morning, and make the necessary adjustments to the presentation. My job was safe and, more importantly, our marriage survived the conflict.

We have gotten it right:

Recently, we're in the season of adjusting to both of our young adult children being married. We are grateful for their marriages and intentional about honoring their independence and time with their spouses. This is something we are unified on. And though I know that it is not our responsibility (or our place, even) to invite them every time we do something fun, my heart still feels a little guilty when Rob and I plan something for just the two of us. Rob has loved me well by patiently acknowledging my feelings. And I've been loving him well by engaging in the planning and the fun.

We are also in a season of transition with our aging bodies. We are working as a team to love and support one another as we embrace each new season. Isn't it remarkable? After all this time, we are still learning!

And just tonight, when I was "on a roll" here, Rob offered to take care of dinner so that I could keep writing, even though he was tired from working hard on a project all day.

> *Love is possible when we are walking in surrender to the Spirit.*

EXPLORE THESE PASSAGES

- 1 Corinthians Chapter 13
- Matthew 22:34-40
- 1 John 4:7-19
- Romans 8:35-39

REFLECT AND DISCUSS

1. What attribute of God's love, listed in 1 Corinthians 13 helps you feel closest to Him and why?
2. How could you love your spouse in that way?
3. What can make it difficult to love like that?
4. What would walking in surrender to the Spirit look like in your marriage?

Chapter Two

JOY

Joy is a deep sense of "it is well" that is not diminished in difficult circumstances. Joy is closely tied to hope. It is possible to have Joy on the darkest days when our hope is healthy. Hope is something we need to feed.

How do we feed our hope? Of first importance is putting our hope in the right place. While there is nothing wrong with hoping that God will bring an improvement in our circumstances, placing our hope *in* "improved circumstances" is not the way to go. In order for hope to be strong, it needs to be anchored in something unchanging, like the Goodness of God, the Power of God, and His Loving Nature. These things remain and are never in dispute or disrepair. They are set in stone. Reliable.

Feeding my hope happens when I choose to take in and receive His Word like a hungry person devours a hearty meal. It happens when I choose to spend time with other Christ followers who will point me to God no matter what is going on.

Another important step to finding Joy is focusing on God's Goodness. Believing and trusting that God is good and is working for our good in all things makes Joy possible.

What does this look like in the context of marriage? Good question. Have you ever looked at your spouse across the table and thought, "God, help me!"? That's the first step. (I just laughed out loud a little bit while typing that, but I'm not kidding.) Some days, some months...maybe even some years in a lifelong marriage are going to be difficult. And some may even feel impossible. That's not an exaggeration; it's the truth. With us humans, some things *are* impossible, but with God, all things are possible. (Jesus said that.)

It may be impossible to experience Joy in your marriage some days in your own strength. But because of Jesus, we're not doing this in our own strength. So, begin with prayer - invite the Creator of the Universe to help you. It's the perfect way to move toward Joy. This is where trusting, meditating, and believing in God's Goodness come in.

When I look at my husband through the lens of God's Goodness, I can trust that God put him specifically in my life. Some days, this provision may be for my comfort and protection. Some days, this provision may be for my growth in areas I'm lacking - maybe patience? Our spouses are God's gifts to us, not to just have fun with. Often, this closest personal relationship helps us grow in our faith by exercising our faith. God has never plopped down a perfect spouse so that the recipient could have an easy life. That's not the way "being human" works. If you have fallen for the lie that some people are experiencing this reality and you are somehow the only one "cursed" with a marriage that takes work, you're mistaken. Granted, some personality types get along more easily than others, and some people have more practice at being married so it looks easier. But trust me, your great marriage will be worth the work that it will require!

There's hope for all of us.

When we were just a few years into our marriage (we were still in our early twenties at the time), a coworker commented to me that she admired the way her father-in-law treated her mother-in-law and she wished her husband and her marriage were more like what she saw in theirs. She had said so to her mother-in-law who replied, "Oh, Honey. It wasn't always like this. We've just gotten better at it."

That has stuck with me. And with each year that has passed, I have seen this coming true in my own marriage. But it's not just "happening" - just like running a marathon doesn't just "happen." There are grueling workouts and hanging in there during dry or stormy seasons, and offering grace and forgiveness (and receiving grace and forgiveness) again and again.

> ***Joy is possible when we are walking in surrender to the Spirit.***

EXPLORE THESE PASSAGES

- Psalm 19:8
- Proverbs 27:19
- Romans 15:13
- James 1:2-4

REFLECT AND DISCUSS

1. Who are the most joyful people you know? What habits and rhythms do you see in their lives?
2. When have you experienced Joy despite difficult circumstances? How did the Lord help you persevere and fill you with hope?
3. What does your spouse need from you in the area of Joy?
4. What would walking in surrender to the Spirit look like in your marriage?

THE SECRET IS IN SURRENDER · 23

Chapter 3

PEACE

The Peace of God is a quiet feeling of assurance deep inside regardless of what is happening around you - a quietness of the soul. A still confidence within. But how about Peace between people - it is merely the absence of conflict? Some people believe Peace means always agreeing, but it goes deeper and is much more lovely than that. God's Peace between people is about the presence of unity in the face of disagreement and differing opinions.

What are the markers of Peace (the presence of unity) in a relationship? First, there's steadiness and a knowing that anything is "work-through-able," so there's not the pressure that would come from the threat of the relationship ending. Peace is also long-haul thinking and actively bringing Peace by planning ahead (not in a manipulative sort of way, but in a loving sort of way). For example: when you know that the two of you have different feelings about a topic, you can intentionally plan to accommodate the other's feelings rather than plotting how you can win and get your way. It is working together to keep things in the peace zone.

Peace entails a calm demeanor and gentle words even when our feelings aren't quite there yet. This is not to be phony, but to show how much we value one another. It's caring more about the other person and your marriage than being "right." This was a doozy for me to learn. By nature (I am a firstborn, wired for order, details, and accuracy), I am intentional and precise about most things. So, if there's a detail to recall, I usually can. I'm the one my parents and my brother ask when they have a question about "What year did we....?" "Was so-and-so there when ...?" "What did we have for dinner when we bought the station wagon?" (By the way, the night we purchased our brand-new 1972 blue Plymouth Fury station wagon, we ate at a Howard Johnson's near the NJ Turnpike). It's not just my family of origin. Rob asks me for people's names and details all the time. I'm sort of like my family's encyclopedia of facts, names and trivia. When there's a question that needs to be answered, I've usually got it, correctly.

This carries over to matters of opinion or the best way to approach a project; I can give a list of reasons why there's a "best way." It can be really hard for me NOT to be condescending about other ideas when I'm sure about mine. As you can imagine, this has caused quite a bit of conflict over the years.

(Yes, I realize how awful I sound right now. How do I have any friends?!)

I know my tendencies, so I work extra hard to be agreeable. As a person who values Peace (unity, but also easy, non-confrontational conversations), I have developed a habit of phrasing my opinions as questions rather than as statements to avoid sounding bossy. Instead of saying "Let's go to the pool" I'll ask, "Do you want to go to the pool?" Instead of "I need your help with the dishes," I might ask, "Want to help me wash these dishes?" I know what you're thinking, and of course, you're right! I DO need to work on communicating more clearly! That became more obvious than ever after one of the most frustrating arguments caused by this idiosyncrasy of mine.

We had been taking care of our friends' dog. A few hours before they were due to return home from their trip, we dropped the dog off at their house. I asked, "Should we leave Zoe out of her crate?" And Rob said, "No, let's leave her in her crate." But since I asked that question already having a strong idea of what I thought was "right" and "best" for Zoe, I trampled over his answer, and it didn't go well.

We were both operating in good faith, but neither of us was using enough words to express the beliefs and emotions we had behind our opinions, and we got locked up real tight, real fast. Feelings were hurt and intelligences were insulted. Once we calmed down (and it took a really long time!) I learned that when I ask for Rob's opinion, but then disregard it and do it my way anyway, it is hurtful. If I had said, "Cinda said we can leave Zoe out of her crate, so that's what I think we should do." He could have just agreed or countered with "but I will feel bad if Zoe has an accident in their house, and she also said she can be in her crate for a few hours, so I think we should leave her in the crate." We could have had a healthy discussion and made a good decision together.

I have learned (by failing miserably at it for a long time) that Rob's feelings should be a higher priority than proving my point, even when my point is valid and my motives are pure. If I'm a person of Peace, I need to be a person of Peace in all circumstances. This is when being a long-haul thinker comes into play. When we get locked into an argument and leave the place of Peace, it is more difficult to hear what the other person is saying or to understand what they are intending to say. It is less likely that we will be able to ask clarifying questions that would lead to understanding. It is harder to give the benefit of the doubt and to believe the best about one another.

Here's some good news: when we trust the Holy Spirit to guide us, we do not have to be frantic or anxious about getting our way; instead, we will be better able to discern God's way.

Peace is worth pursuing, so keep at it! When your marriage displays this kind of unity, you will be grateful, and the positive impact will extend to future generations, whether they are raised in your home or nearby.

> ***Peace is possible when we are walking in surrender to the Spirit.***

EXPLORE THESE PASSAGES

- Psalm 23
- Isaiah 26:3
- Romans 8:5-6
- Romans 12:14-18

REFLECT AND DISCUSS

1. Where/when have you felt the most peaceful?
2. What does it look like for you to struggle in this area?
3. Which verses in Psalm 23 give you hope that Peace is possible? Explain.
4. What would walking in surrender to the Spirit look like in your marriage?

Chapter Four

PATIENCE

If you have ever thought, "I'm just not a very patient person," you are not alone. Most of us, by nature, are not patient people. We don't get Patience by praying for it and then having it magically bestowed upon us. We all need to exercise Patience. Just like all the other Fruit of the Spirit, it is something that becomes more true of us as we exercise it. And we exercise it by denying ourselves and placing our desires (for quick action or faster answers or for the person in front of us in the grocery line to stop being so dang friendly to the cashier) on the back burner. It doesn't get easier with practice; we just get better at it. We begin to understand the power in it. I don't mean "power" in the manipulative, "winning" sense of the word. I mean the power to glorify God, the power to successfully navigate a difficult situation, and the ability to set the tone for positive outcomes in the face of trying times.

Patience is not wimpy or weak. It's quite the opposite. Patience requires brute strength of character - self-control "like you mean it." Waiting patiently, loving patiently, speaking patiently when you're in the thick of it - all of these take tremendous effort, restraint, and absolute surrender. Working through the misunderstandings and treating one another with respect until you arrive at a solution can take a lot of Patience.

Falling asleep peacefully when you haven't yet arrived at the solution and carrying on with all of the daily things while continuing to work toward resolution take Patience.

A practical example:

A few years ago, it was time to decide about our family vacation. It was the last summer before our son was getting married, so even though it wouldn't be the last time we'd ever take a vacation together, we knew it would be the last trip as a family of four. We live on the east coast and had dreamed for years of taking the kids with us to San Francisco. Budget is a big factor in our vacation planning ("ministry salaries" - If you know, you know!) and most of our vacation destinations are drivable. Our budget for that summer's trip was not going to get us to San Francisco.

But then, we got an unexpected tax refund. Immediately, I thought, "Yes! San Fran!" Also immediately, Rob thought, "Yes! Build up the savings account because we're going to need an A/C unit soon!"

I'm guessing that if you and your spouse are reading this together, each of you relates strongly to one of these gut reactions - but not the same one. That's just the way God usually matches us up.

Rob is the one who watches over our finances, so he feels the weight of saving for an emergency more than I do. We were in a good spot to work through this due to some learning we had done on communication and problem solving, and because we chose to surrender to the Holy Spirit. We both approached this decision with robust Patience. We had level-headed conversations. We were able to see ourselves on the same team, and we were able to wait it out and sort through our emotions and fears in an objective way.

This means that my "what if we never get this chance again?" as well as Rob's "what if the A/C craps out and we need a roof and get a really big car repair bill after we order airline tickets?" were both acknowledged with respect and proper perspective. Neither of us rushed to defend our views. We were able to wait until we could get through the fear of "losing" something. We addressed all the feelings. We believed the best in one another.

I was able to honestly say, "I am going to have a great time no matter where we go. If we decide not to go to San Francisco, I am not going to be upset or bitter. I don't want you to have to feel worried about finances, so I'm comfortable with whatever you decide. I value your peace of mind more than a vacation." (This is not my nature, as you've read above. See how lovely the Holy Spirit is?) This freed Rob up to not worry about disappointing me. And that freedom allowed him the breathing room he needed. Within a few minutes, he called Elizabeth and Nick to say, "Get excited - we're going to San Francisco!"

Patience can look like deciding in advance to allow the other person's "decider" to catch up when you have differing viewpoints.

As you'd expect, it was an AMAZING trip! We found some great bargains while we were there that helped our money go further than we expected.

Patience is possible when we are walking in surrender to the Spirit.

EXPLORE THESE PASSAGES

- Proverbs 19:11
- Colossians 1:9-14
- Hebrews 6:10-12
- James 5:7-9

REFLECT AND DISCUSS

1. Where have you struggled most with Patience?
2. How has God been patient with you?
3. What would it look like for you to be "strengthened with all God's power" for Patience in your marriage? (Colossians 1:11)
4. What would walking in surrender to the Spirit look like in your marriage?

_____
_____
_____
_____
_____
_____
_____
_____
_____

THE SECRET IS IN SURRENDER

Chapter Five

KINDNESS

What comes to mind when you hear the word KINDNESS?

For me, it's Ephesians 4:32. "Be kind to one another, tenderhearted, forgiving one another, as God in Christ forgave you."

If I am being tender-hearted, I decide in advance that I will believe the best about the other person. The story in my head and in my heart about my husband will be that he is trying his best. I will have tolerance for mistakes and imperfections because I know that even when I'm trying my best, I make mistakes. I will make room for him to be a fallible person. I will not expect perfection.

Something integral here is to learn from our mistakes.

One of my mistakes:

Several years ago, on a vacation to visit my side of the family, we were celebrating my grandparent's 60th anniversary on the night before we were leaving. It was a big part of the reason we had chosen that week for our visit and I was helping with the preparations and was in charge of the cake for the party. With two young kids, it was a big undertaking. Amid all the activity of getting ready for the party and setting up, in addition to baking and decorating a large two-tiered stacked cake, there were a lot of decisions to be made. I wanted it to be perfect. I had left Rob in charge of getting the kids to the party location. I expected that he would show up in a nice casual shirt - like maybe a polo - something with a collar. He arrived in a souvenir t-shirt that he had gotten that day while we were apart. I was surprised (and also, thought the shirt was tacky) and my displeasure was evident on my face and in my tone as I greeted him with, "Nice t-shirt."

When I look back on this, I am embarrassed and dismayed that this was my reaction to seeing my husband and children for the first time in several hours. Sure, I was tired and stressed from all that I had navigated that day. Yes, I was expecting one thing and was met with something different. But on the other side of the coin, he had been caring for our kids that afternoon to make it possible for me to focus on the cake and all the party prep. He was also tired and ready to be together. Instead of greeting him warmly, receiving him the way he was, and expressing my gratitude for the work he had done that allowed me to be on the party committee, I let my circumstances, fatigue, and stress lead my attitude, rather than the Holy Spirit.

His face fell. Then he got defensive, "This isn't good enough for your family?"

Now, let me set the stage. We were about to eat dinner on picnic tables under the pine trees at my grandparents' campground. It was an outdoor event. In the summer. For shade from the sun and any raindrops, we had strung mismatched tarps above the table. It was not a fancy affair. We are not a fancy family. That is what makes my attitude even more unwarranted and embarrassing to admit. Granted, the menu was on the fancy side - we were eating steaks and lobster, and let's just say the cake was delicious and beautiful, but the setting definitely lent itself to t-shirts (even tacky ones) and shorts.

I wish I could say that I asked for forgiveness quickly. I also wish that he'd had the emotional strength to meet my criticism with grace enough to shrug it off, but neither of us could muster it. Instead, I berated myself and we avoided eye contact for most of the evening. Since we were leaving early the next morning, I had to say my goodbyes to beloved family members in a mixed-up state. Looking back, I am ashamed of how badly I missed the point!

My motive for wanting things to be "just right" was pure (to celebrate my grandparents' marriage milestone well), but my idea of what would constitute a good celebration was off-kilter. I put an imaginary dress code ahead of Kindness. Instead of loving my husband well in honor of their marriage, I spoke to him in a way that I don't even speak to people I don't like. Kindness was not something I was even feigning at that moment.

Speaking well of one another is another way to practice Kindness. As wives and husbands, we have a front-row seat to one another's shortcomings and faults. Kindness means that we don't flaunt those things or hold them over one another's heads. Nothing good comes from bad-mouthing one another. Instead of sharing about the negative, imperfect things I've done this week or the ways I have let him down, Rob has the choice of sharing about the positives in public. This is different than sharing a false representation of perfection on social media, setting others up for dashed expectations or ideas about what a good marriage looks like, but you've heard the wisdom "If you can't say something nice, don't say anything at all, right? That's Kindness.

Let's take a look at what the Bible says just before the verse about Kindness and being tender-hearted. Ephesians 4:30-31 sets us up for verse 32 by showing us what Kindness is NOT and also, what the source of our success will be:

"And do not grieve the Holy Spirit of God, by whom you were sealed for the day of redemption. Let all bitterness and wrath and anger and clamor and slander be put away from you, along with all malice."

These things that we are to put away (bitterness, wrath, anger, clamor, slander, malice), do not serve our relationships. They are quite the opposite of Kindness. If you have any questions about whether you're doing well with Kindness, think through this list and examine yourself. Check your motives and attitude often, and ask for forgiveness quickly when you need to.

Kindness is possible when we are walking in surrender to the Spirit.

EXPLORE THESE PASSAGES

- Jeremiah 9:24
- Ephesians 4:29-32
- Colossians 3:12-14
- Titus 3:3-8

REFLECT AND DISCUSS

1. List some examples of when you "got Kindness wrong" and when you "got it right." Knowing what communicates Kindness to our spouses can help us repeat those actions, words, and behaviors.
2. What are some examples of God's grace and mercy in your life? (Titus 3:3-8)
3. How can you take measures to safeguard Kindness in your relationship?
4. What would walking in surrender to the Spirit look like in your marriage?

Chapter 6

GOODNESS

"Wisdom has its root in goodness." Ralph Waldo Emerson

"Do all the good you can and make as little fuss about it as possible." Charles Dickens

"Goodness is the only investment that never fails." Henry David Thoreau

"Goodness" - it seems like it should be easy, right? Especially if the opposite is "badness." But is Goodness really just "not treating each other badly?" That seems like a cop-out.

Maybe the best way to understand how to be good to one another is to look at some ways God is good to us.

- God is intentional - He loved us first and gave His only Son for us. (1 John 4:19, John 3:16)
- God knows the plan He has for us, and it's a plan for our good. (Jeremiah 29:11)
- God blesses us with good things, even when we don't deserve them. (Matthew 5:45)

It doesn't seem like Godly Goodness is only about "not being awful" to one another. We will be making an intentional effort - and investing time, energy, and other resources in one another if we're going to get this right. And don't we all want to get this right?

Goodness entails making one another our top priority. After Jesus, our spouses deserve the next spot on our list. This means making time for one another, communicating well, studying the other to know what they need most, and then finding a way to make it happen.

Goodness means finding ways to serve our spouses and lighten one another's burdens. Goodness means doing things like learning our spouse's love language and expressing our love in the way they receive it best, even when it is difficult or out of our comfort zone. Without having to be reminded.

An example from our marriage:

Winter is a difficult season for me. The short days, the cold, the bare trees - I feel "blah" quite a bit. Several years ago, Rob took stock of the situation and decided to do something about it. He did some research and bought tickets to a concert in March that he knew I would love. This was his gift to me at Christmas. We planned a fun family trip that I could then look forward to all winter. Every year since, he has found ways to make winter more bearable and he goes out of his way to make sure there is something fun to look forward to. It helps me get through the difficult season and it also makes me feel incredibly loved and cared for.

Goodness means making allowances for one another's weaknesses. You are strong in ways your spouse is not. So, bring your best every day. Don't be lured into thinking marriage is a 50/50 deal. It is not as if you get married and then only have to bring 50% of yourself. That is a flawed understanding. On your best days, marriage will be 100/100 - both of you bringing your best. Even when you do, it will not feel like 100/100. You may be tired, hungry and possibly even "hangry." Illness might befall one of you. On the days when one of you is truly struggling, if you both commit to bringing all that you have, you may feel like between both of you, you've still got a failing grade, but you know what? Bringing all that you can on the given day, whether it's an easy one or a tough one, is what Goodness is all about. We can trust that God is always there to make it more than it is.

> ***Goodness is possible when we are walking in surrender to the Spirit.***

EXPLORE THESE PASSAGES

- Psalm 23
- Psalm 145:1-7
- Psalm 100:5
- James 1:17
- 2 Peter 1:3-8

REFLECT AND DISCUSS

1. Name a friend or family member who has a handle on "Goodness." What do you admire about the way God works through them?
2. Share a time when you felt or experienced the Goodness of God through something done or said by your spouse.
3. What can you do to support your spouse's spiritual growth?
4. What would walking in surrender to the Spirit look like in your marriage?

Chapter 7

FAITHFULNESS

Faithfulness in marriage is certainly about fidelity - about keeping your marriage bed pure (and also healthy!), but it is not solely about that.

Faithfulness is about doing what you say you will do, when you say you will do it. Faithfulness is about being trustworthy and reliable. Being a person of integrity, whom your spouse can count on. Being a dependable person.

Faithfulness is also about making one another (and your marriage) your first priority. This can look like checking with your spouse when you're invited to something to make sure it will work for your relationship, not just your individual calendar. It's about prioritizing and committing to the things that you've decided to do as a couple to reach the goals you've set as a couple.

Faithfulness keeps the dreams and hopes for the future at the forefront today so things stay on track and dreams have a chance of being fulfilled and goals can be met tomorrow. If you've been tempted to think that someone who has "freedom to do whatever they want" has it better than you, change your thinking. That relationship is likely doomed. Even if things look okay, it may just be hanging on by a thin thread.

Budgeting is something we struggled with for many years. It's not that we lived beyond our means, as far as our regular monthly expenses were concerned, but we had no plan for emergencies or those "once a year" expenses, like Christmas or vacation. Consequently, when we were Christmas shopping or on vacation, (or when a vehicle needed tires), things were much more stressful and conflict-ridden than they needed to be. They say budgeting is you telling your money where it should go, rather than it telling you where it went. It's the same with marriage. When we decide in advance what we're working toward, we are more likely to get there.

Being happily married is not sunshine and rainbows all the time. Anything that rubs you the wrong way is an opportunity to grow - personally, spiritually, emotionally, and relationally! A happy marriage is one where we are faithfully working and growing through the challenging bits together. We're supporting one another in that growth. And there's grace in abundance for when we don't get it totally right.

Faithfulness entails commitment and discipline - much like workouts and training for athletes, the educational rigor involved in pursuing an advanced degree, and the stamina and dedication involved in building a business or planting a church. But it is not only about bearing down with all your strength. It is about humbling ourselves to the Spirit's guidance and direction - allowing ourselves to be transformed into faithful people.

A good marriage requires intentionality, tenacity, and surrender to God's leadership. A lifelong marriage is built one moment, one day at a time. And it is worth the investment.

Faithfulness is possible when we are walking in surrender to the Spirit.

EXPLORE THESE PASSAGES

- Psalm 26
- Proverbs 3:3
- 1 Corinthians 10:31
- Psalm 36:5

REFLECT AND DISCUSS

1. What evidence of the Lord's Faithfulness have you experienced?
2. List some ways you are already practicing Faithfulness.
3. On a scale of 1-10, how trustworthy are you and your spouse?
4. What would walking in surrender to the Spirit look like in your marriage?

_____
_____
_____
_____
_____
_____
_____
_____
_____
_____
_____

Chapter 8

GENTLENESS

Who in your life would you describe as gentle? Is their Gentleness more about being physically gentle or being emotionally gentle - meaning, is their voice quiet and their movement graceful and non-intrusive, or is it more a matter of them using gentle words and being considerate of the hearts, souls, and spirits of others? Something in between?

When I think of "Gentleness," it is closely tied with Patience. Because for me to be gentle with another person's feelings, especially at times when I am frustrated, a good deal of Patience must be exerted. "Exerting Patience" sounds like an oxymoron, but it is truly a feat to filter out my anger and frustration in certain instances to get the desired result of Gentleness. For me, it is as if Gentleness is the physical representation of internal Patience.

Gentleness can also be thought of in terms of the impact of our existence. "Leave only footprints" is a way we can be gentle with the earth when we visit a park. "Leave only encouragement" might be the way we'd say it in terms of marriage.

If I follow the adage to leave a place better than I find it, how much more so should I act this way in my relationships and, especially, in my marriage? When I find my spouse in a position of needing something (help, encouragement, a break, some rest, some fun, intimacy) if I walk on by without offering what I can, that is NOT Gentleness.

Criticism and name-calling are obvious foes to Gentleness, and so are eye rolls, stink eye, and "wandering eye."

Gentleness involves being a soft place to land. Gentleness is going to require listening - a lot of listening. Listen, listen, listen. Go beyond what you can hear and listen with your heart to your spouse. Do you hear fatigue? Find a way to encourage her to rest. Do you hear he is at his wit's end? It is time to quickly find a way to help him keep going forward.

When it comes to your spouse, it is not "someone else's job" to help him or her find and receive what he/she needs. This does not mean that you are responsible to meet every need, but if you have access to help or blessing and withhold it, you do a disservice to your marriage.

Let's be the first cheerleaders, the best helpers, the number one advocates, as far as this most important of human relationships is concerned. Anything less is not what Jesus desires for our marriages. It just isn't.

Gentleness in our marriage looks like this: speaking words that build one another up and choosing the right time and place to share the truth in love. Here's some excellent wisdom that you may also have heard: "Praise in public, correct in private." (This is key for parenting as well.)

An example from our marriage:

We haven't always been great communicators in times of conflict and stress, but a few years ago, we were having a disagreement and some words popped out of my mouth that hadn't been well-chosen or even really thought out. I don't remember what we were even discussing or what the words were. What I do remember is the way Rob offered me grace and a second chance. He gently said, "That sounds harsh." It diffused the situation quickly. He could have fired back his own set of words. He could have gotten defensive. He could have wagged a finger at me telling me I was wrong. Instead, he spoke the truth gently, giving me the benefit of the doubt and the chance to back up a bit and choose a better way to express my feelings.

Even though Gentleness is not a strong suit for many of us humans, it is part of the Fruit of the Spirit. That means that as Christ followers, our lives can be marked by Gentleness.

> *Gentleness is possible when we are walking in surrender to the Spirit.*

EXPLORE THESE PASSAGES

- Isaiah 40:11
- Ephesians 4:2-6
- Colossians 3:1-16 (especially v. 12)
- 1 Timothy 6:11

REFLECT AND DISCUSS

1. What words would you use to describe the Lord's Gentleness?
2. What changes you can begin making today to be more gentle with your spouse?
3. What are some ways you could benefit from the Gentleness of your spouse?
4. What would walking in surrender to the Spirit look like in your marriage?

THE SECRET IS IN SURRENDER

Chapter 9

SELF-CONTROL

Self-control goes hand in hand with faithfulness and then kicks it up a few levels. And it would be impossible to exhibit Self-control without Patience, but it goes way beyond that; plenty of people seemingly can wait for things well but have deep struggles with Self-control when no one is looking.

Self-control knows how to say, "No." Every single temptation is an opportunity to glorify God. We're talking about marriage here, so Self-control definitely comes into play as it pertains to marital faithfulness, but not every temptation is about an affair. While infidelity can be a death knell to a once-healthy marriage, (I've personally seen some marriages survive it - resurrection power is no joke!) there will also be little temptations to put other things and other people ahead of your spouse. These should also be considered dangerous.

Self-control doesn't shy away from doing hard things and mundane tasks. Self-control helps us deny ourselves and pick up our crosses. It helps us prioritize our marriage. We can give our marriage top billing in lots of big ways and many small ways. Some examples are the calendar and finances. We can plan ahead to protect our marriage. Together, we can decide in advance which nights are "off limits" as far as scheduling outside commitments and then honor that decision. We can make a plan and budget money for the things our "us-ness" needs - things like vacations, resources, and retreats that will encourage, strengthen, and enrich our relationship.

One of the things I respect about Rob is that he is a man of integrity. What you see is what you get with him. He consistently chooses the high road. He's not perfect, but his motives are pure and he is honest. He's solid. (He also has the sense of humor of a middle school boy, and he will giggle about potty humor no matter who is in the room.) Integrity and Self-control go hand-in-hand. A person of integrity is the same whether they are in public or in private. Self-control is the pathway to integrity. Self-control keeps our spouse safe physically and emotionally.

Don't be a flake - be a person of your word. If you tell your spouse that you're available for something they need your help with, honor that. If you get invited to something fun with your friends or co-workers on a day you've agreed that you reserve for each other, just say no. Don't discount the powerful example you can be to others by saying, "Sorry, that's date night, so I'll need to take a rain check."

Something to chew on: the way we respect our spouses and our marriages may be the most powerful aspect of our leadership at home, at work, and in the community. We all have plenty of examples of people who ended up losing their marriages because they put their careers or hobbies ahead of their spouses. If you're on that path yourself, decide right now to change course. It will be worth it!

> ***Self-control is possible when we are walking in surrender to the Spirit.***

EXPLORE THESE PASSAGES

- Proverbs 16:32
- Proverbs 25:28
- 2 Timothy 1:7
- 2 Peter 1:3-12

READ AND REFLECT

1. Rewrite Proverbs 16:32 and 25:28 in your own words.
2. What are some things you can affirm in one another as it pertains to Self-control?
3. List some areas for growth and improvement.
4. What would walking in surrender to the Spirit look like in your marriage?

_____

_____

_____

_____

_____

_____

_____

_____

_____

_____

Chapter 10

WE ARE JUST BEGINNING

You've made it here. Great job, Friend!

I pray that you are having great experiences in trusting God and that you are seeing God move in your heart as you surrender to the leading of His Holy Spirit. Marriage is a lifelong journey with the potential to be both life-giving and full of rich blessings. It is not easy, that's for sure. It is, however, worth it. Just as with all aspects of life, when we release our death grip and invite God to take control, we get better. In this case, our marriages get better and we'll find that we get better at being married. We will see things that were "not possible" in our own strength become possible because of God's strength. When we attempt to do them in our own strength, it isn't sustainable. We get tired and frustrated and start to exhibit the fruit of the flesh. God's power to save and transform cannot be overestimated! I pray that you are more surrendered to the leading of the Holy Spirit and more committed than ever to making your marriage the best it can be.

When we walk in a surrendered way, we will exhibit the fruit of the Holy Spirit. Our marriages (and all other relationships, really) will be stronger, and happier and we'll bear the healthy fruit of Love, Joy, Peace, Patience, Kindness, Goodness, Faithfulness, Gentleness, and Self-control.

The best part: God will get all the Glory.

Before you set this book aside and move on to whatever's next, take a moment to look back through - which attributes of the Fruit of the Spirit are easiest or most natural for you? Celebrate those! Thank God for how He's wired you and for all the progress you have already made.

Which are the most challenging? You may want to go back and spend more time on those - not to become perfect (none of us is going to get there) - but truly, don't miss the chance for God to do even more in your heart.

I am praying for you and cheering you on.

Most importantly, God is FOR you. He is FOR your marriage.

THE MOST IMPORTANT SURRENDER

This book is written for married people who follow Jesus. Deciding to accept the gift of salvation that is available through Him is the way a person receives the Holy Spirit in the first place. If you have never made that decision, the concepts contained here will likely sound very strange; foolish, even. The Jesus-following life is certainly counter-cultural. That's why it's impossible to exhibit the fruit of the Spirit without the Spirit.

There must be a reason that you turned to this page, even if it is simply curiosity. You may have landed here because you're hoping that God will help your marriage be better. You're still holding the book and still reading, so I'm taking that as permission to invite you to consider that forgiveness and a new life are available to you through Jesus.

Why would you need forgiveness? You're probably a very nice person. I'm guessing you do your best and have never intentionally hurt anyone. The trouble is that none of us is good enough to earn our way into Heaven. We can never do enough good deeds or avoid all the bad stuff perfectly.

Romans 6:23 (NIV): For the wages of sin is death, but the gift of God is eternal life in Christ Jesus our Lord.

Our good deeds fall short and only earn us death, not eternal life with God. The condition of our sin (we're born sinful and selfish and if you have any doubts about that, just take a toy away from a 2-year-old) separates us from God. Go back and look at Galatians 5:19-21. This list is just a sampling of our sinful condition. You and I desire the fruit of the Spirit in our marriage because we sin and experience the opposite of what we desire. There is Hope. I've got wonderful news. Ready for it?

God loves you. That's right, He does!

Say it out loud: "God loves me."

He created you with all your uniqueness and has known every detail of your life, even the sin, since before you were even conceived. Because He desires to have a relationship with you, he made a way for the forgiveness of your sins - past, present and future. Jesus, his Son, who is the only person (Jesus was fully human and fully God) without sin, offered his life as a sacrifice to cover your sin - to pay the penalty on your behalf, and reconcile you to your Heavenly Father. John 3:16 (NIV): For God so loved the world that he gave his one and only Son, that whoever believes in him shall not perish but have eternal life.

You're still here, Friend. Here on this page, and here on the Earth. There is so much more I'd like to tell you, but I want to simply invite you to step into faith - you can start following Jesus right now. It's as easy as A-B-C:

> **Admit** *your need for forgiveness - stop trying to earn your way to God.*
>
> **Believe** *that Jesus is the Son of God and that his death paid the full price for your sin.*
>
> **Commit** *to learning more and to following him with the rest of your life.*

What now?

Philippians 1:6 (NIV): being confident of this, that he who began a good work in you will carry it on to completion until the day of Christ Jesus.

It will be important for you to share this decision with someone. The Holy Spirit is a gift given to everyone who makes this decision - He will guide and comfort you, and because He wants to make sure God gets the glory for this, you're going to feel "nudged" to share this decision. It will also be important to start growing in your understanding of who God is and what H/e wants for your life. Reading the Bible (get the YouVersion App!), and finding a good church will be key.

If you have no idea where to start on those things, will you send me an email? I'd love to be able to pray for you and help you take the next step in your journey!

kimberlyjoanperry@gmail.com

www.ingramcontent.com/pod-product-compliance
Lightning Source LLC
Chambersburg PA
CBHW060352050426
42449CB00011B/2939